Usborne Englis

Level 1

Puss
IN
Boots

Retold by Mairi Mackinnon

Illustrated by Gemma Román

English language consultant: Peter Viney

# Contents

You can listen to the story online here:
www.usborneenglishreaders.com/
pussinboots

There was once a poor man who had three sons. He had a small farm, and a donkey and a cat, and nothing else in the world.

Before he died, he gave the farm to his oldest son. He gave the donkey to his next son. He looked sadly at Tom, the youngest. "I'm sorry, all I have left is the cat."

Tom tried to smile. "That's all right, Father. Puss is very clever, I know. He always catches lots of mice."

But when his father was dead, Tom knew that he couldn't stay at home. His brothers could work together on the farm with the donkey, but they didn't need him.

"What can I do with a cat?" he asked. "I can't even eat him."

"Eat me?" answered Puss. "Oh, please don't do that. I have a much better idea. Give me a cloak and a hat and some boots, and I think I can help you."

Tom was surprised, but he found the clothes for Puss. Then Puss put them on.

"Puss, you look amazing!" said Tom.

Puss took off his hat and bowed. "Thank you, master." Next, he picked up a bag and some carrots and went into the forest. Puss left the bag on the ground with the carrots in it. He hid behind a tree and waited.

Soon, two young rabbits came out to eat the carrots. Puss jumped out and caught them. Then he put them in the bag.

He went to the King's palace. "I have a present for the King," he said, "from my master, the Marquis of Carabas."

"The Marquis of Carabas? Never heard of him." A servant took the rabbits, and Puss waited.

Soon the servant came back. "The King says thank you for his present," he said. "Your master is very kind."

The next day, Puss went into a field. He left his bag on the ground with some corn in it, and waited. Soon, four fat little birds came to eat the corn. Puss jumped out and caught them. Then he put them in the bag.

He went back to the King's palace. "I have another present," he said. Again, the King said thank you, and the servant gave Puss a few coins.

"Puss, you are the cleverest cat in the world," said Tom. That night, he and Puss had a good dinner.

"Oh, this is nothing," said Puss. "Next week, the King is going out in his carriage with his daughter, the Princess. You must do as I tell you."

Every day, Puss took another present to the palace. The next week, he took Tom to the river and told him to go swimming. Then he hid Tom's old clothes.

Soon he saw the King's carriage, and he jumped into the road. "Help! Help!" he said. "My poor master, the Marquis of Carabas! Some robbers attacked him and took all his clothes!"

"The Marquis of Carabas?" said the King. "He gave me all those nice presents. Oh, that's terrible!" He sent a servant to bring some clothes from the palace.

When Tom put them on, he looked just like a prince. The Princess smiled at him. She was very pretty.

"Please, dear Marquis," said the King.
"Would you like to ride with us in our
carriage? And your cat, too?"

"Thank you," said Puss, "but I'm happy
to walk."

He came to some fields of corn.
Some people were cutting the corn.

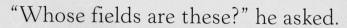

"Whose fields are these?" he asked.

"Oh, they belong to a terrible giant," the people told him.

"They don't now," said Puss. "The King is coming. You must tell him that all these fields belong to the Marquis of Carabas."

"But…"

"Do you want to be cat food?" asked Puss, angrily.

So when the King came, he heard that all the fields belonged to the Marquis.

"Amazing!" said the King. "My dear Marquis, I can see you are a rich man."

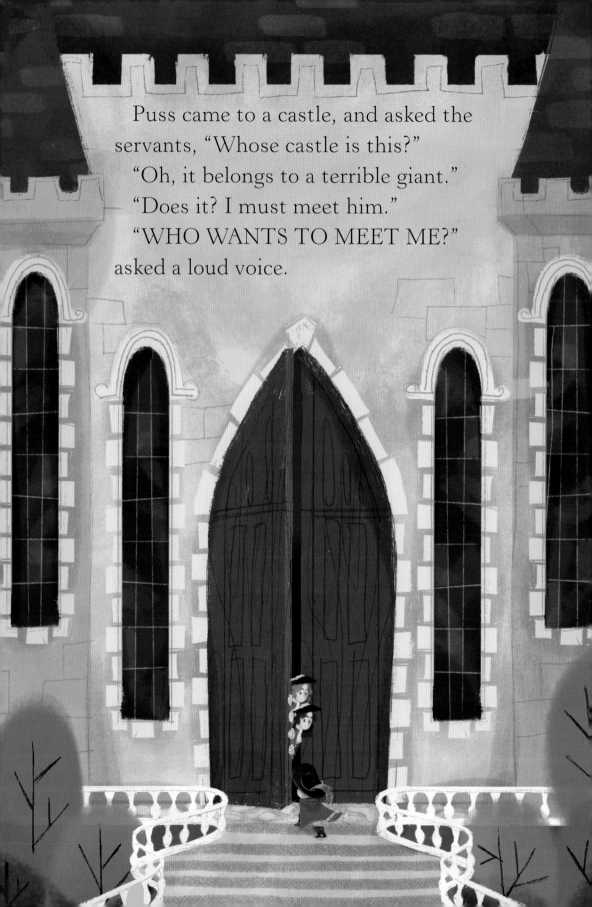

Puss came to a castle, and asked the
servants, "Whose castle is this?"

"Oh, it belongs to a terrible giant."

"Does it? I must meet him."

"WHO WANTS TO MEET ME?"
asked a loud voice.

Puss looked up. The giant was
enormous and very ugly.

"Ah, Mr. Giant," he said. "What a
beautiful castle you have. And all those
cornfields, and so many people working
for you."

"WHAT DO YOU WANT?" asked
the giant.

"Mr. Giant, I heard a story that you can change into any animal — a dog, a cat, or even a lion. Can it be true?"

"OF COURSE IT'S TRUE!" The giant changed into an enormous lion. Puss was very frightened, but he didn't move.

"That's good!" he said. "But can you also change into a really small animal? Like a mouse?"

"EASY!" said the giant, and he changed into a little mouse in front of Puss. Puss jumped on the mouse… and that was the end of the giant.

Just then, the King's carriage arrived. Puss bowed. "Welcome to my master's castle," he said.

"Is this castle yours too?" the King asked. Tom smiled.

"Please, come inside," said Puss. "I'm sure you are hungry." They went into the castle and found a delicious meal all ready on the table.

"Amazing!" said the King. He asked Puss all about his master the Marquis, his castle and his fields and farms. Tom talked to the Princess. She listened to him, and smiled and laughed.

"Tell me, Puss," said the King. "Is your master married?"

"Well, no, he isn't," said Puss.

"I think my daughter likes him very much," said the King. "Is that true, my dear?" The princess went pink. "Yes, I do," she said.

So Tom married the King's daughter,
and they lived in the castle and were
very happy. Puss lived in the castle with
them. He didn't have to catch mice… but
sometimes he did anyway, just for fun.

# About the story

*Puss in Boots* is a story by Charles Perrault. Perrault lived in France from 1628-1703. For most of his life, he worked for the French government, but he was always very interested in books and stories too. In 1695, Perrault lost his government job and started writing stories for his children. *Puss in Boots* is one of these. Perrault took the idea from an older Italian story, but he added some of the best parts – Puss's boots, and also the giant.

Perrault's stories were soon very popular, not only in France but all over Europe. Today, people know and love these stories all around the world. This kind of story is called a fairy story. Fairy stories are often about kings, queens, princes and princesses, fairies and magic. Other fairy stories by Perrault include *Cinderella*, *Little Red Riding Hood* and *Sleeping Beauty*.

# Activities

The answers are on page 32.

## What happened when?

Can you put these pictures and sentences
in the right order?

A.

"Do you want to
be cat food?"

B.

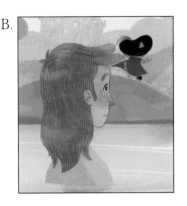

"Some robbers
attacked him and
took all his clothes!"

C.

"Is your master
married?"

D.

Tom knew that he
couldn't stay at home.

E.

Puss jumped on the
mouse... and that was
the end of the giant.

F.

"The King says
thank you."

# What are they thinking?

Choose the right sentence for each person.

A.

I want to help Tom.

B.

I like Tom very much.

C.

The Marquis is a rich man.

D.

What can I do with a cat?

The King          The Princess          Tom          Puss

# What happened next?

Choose the right sentence.

1.

A. The rabbits ate all the carrots.

B. Puss caught the rabbits.

A. Puss rode in the carrriage.

B. Tom rode in the carriage.

2.

3.

A. Puss ate the giant.

B. The giant ate Puss.

# What are they like?

Choose the right word to finish each sentence.

> frightened    clever    sad    delicious
>
> amazing    poor    kind    hungry

1.

"Puss is very ............"

2.

"You look ............"

3.

"My ............ master, the
Marquis of Carabas!"

4.

"I'm sure you are ............"

# A clever cat

One word in each sentence is wrong.
Can you choose the right word instead?

1.

"I have a game for the King."

story   present   word

2.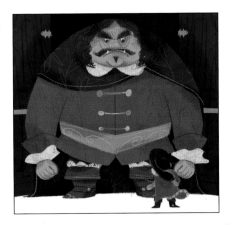

"What a small castle you have."

beautiful   new   magic

3.

"Welcome to my master's house."

castle   garden   forest

4.

"Mr. Giant, I wanted a story."

heard   loved   watched

# Word list

**amazing** (adj) really good, or surprising in a good way.

**arrive** (v) to come to a place after a journey.

**attack** (v) if you attack someone, you start a fight with them.

**belong** (v) if something belongs to you, it is yours.

**boot** (n) something that you wear on your foot. It covers your foot and part of your leg.

**bow** (v) when you bow, you lean forward from your middle to show that a person is more important than you.

**carriage** (n) something that you ride in. In the past, carriages were pulled by horses.

**carrot** (n) a type of orange vegetable. Carrots grow underground.

**cloak** (n) a type of large coat without arms. A cloak covers most of your body.

**coin** (n) a small piece of money.

**corn** (n) corn grows on farms, in fields. You use it to make flour and bread.

**dear** (adj) you say 'dear' to a person you like very much.

**delicious** (adj) very good to eat.

**donkey** (n) an animal like a horse, with long ears. Donkeys are strong and can work hard.